Numbers 1

1 Lucky numbers

Use the code 1 for A, 2 for B, etc. to find your 'lucky number' by making a total for your name.

For example: JOHN SMITH

J O H N S M I T H

10+15+8+14+19+13+9+20+8 = 116

Now add digits 1+1+6 = 8

Lucky number . . . 8

2 Find the missing numbers:

a 1, 3, 5, 7, □, 11, 13, □

b 2, 6, 12, 20, □, 42, □

c 1, 4, 9, 16, □, 36, 49, □

d 42, 39, 36, 33, □, 27, □

e 63, 48, 35, 24, □, 8, □, 0

f $\frac{1}{8}$, $\frac{1}{4}$, □, 1, 2, □

g 1, $\frac{4}{2}$, 3, $\frac{16}{4}$, 5, □, □

h $\frac{18}{24}$, $\frac{15}{20}$, $\frac{12}{16}$, □, $\frac{6}{8}$, □

i 180, 90, 60, □, 36, □

Find the missing letters:

j O, T, T, F, F, S, S, □, □, T.

3 Copy and fill in the missing figures:

a
```
   3*
 +*09
   64
 ----
  3*8
```

b
```
  296
 - 3*
 ----
  **2
```

c
```
  13*
 +*06
  464
 ----
  8*0
```

d
```
  163
 - *8
 ----
   7*
```

e
```
  2*7
 +36*
  *85
 ----
  826
```

f
```
  50*
 -*67
 ----
   *6
```

Shapes 1

1 Cut two triangles of the same shape and size from a piece of card.

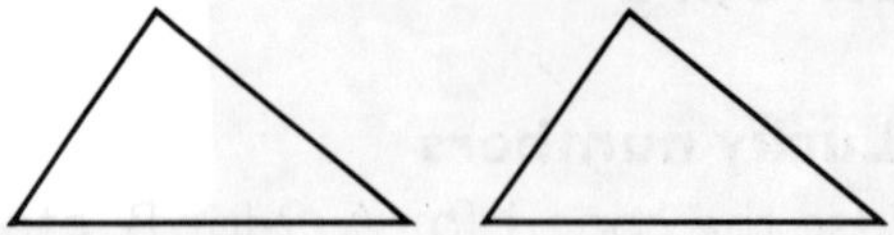

Fit them together to form a parallelogram.

Cut this parallelogram with a single cut and then use the pieces to make a rectangle.

Try again with other pairs of triangles,

for example:

or

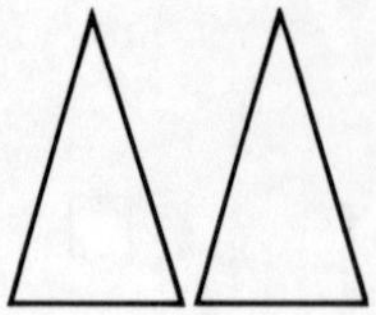

or

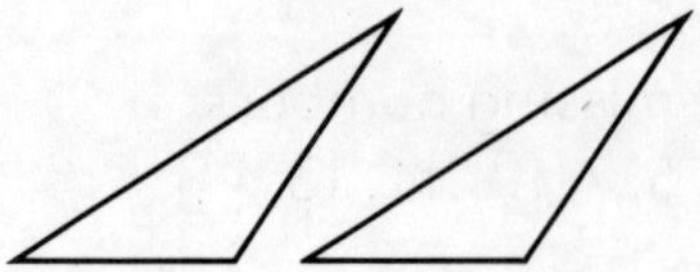

2 What is the smallest number of square tiles all the same size which can be fitted together to form a rectangle in four different ways?
Each rectangle must be of a different shape.

3 Draw a rectangle 10 cm by 5 cm.

Draw a straight line which cuts it in half.
How many different lines can you draw which will cut the rectangle in half?
What do you notice about all of these lines?

4 **The divided farm**
A wealthy farmer with 4 sons owned a three-section farm as shown in this diagram. When he died his will said that the farm should be divided so that each son had $\frac{1}{4}$ of his farm.
He also said that each farm must have the same shape as the original farm.
How was the farm divided?

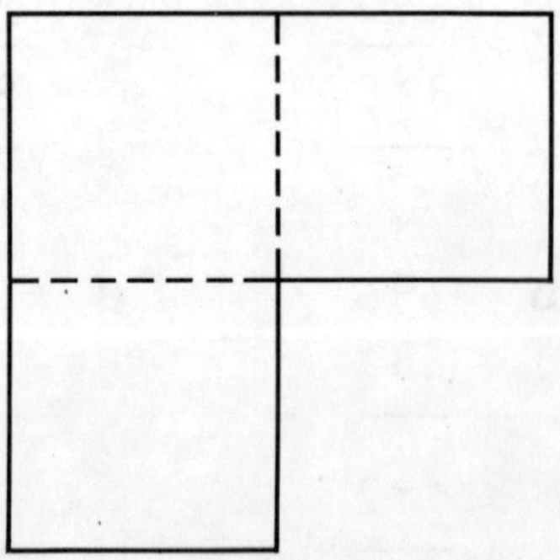

Numbers 2 — 'consecutive'

1 1, 2, 3, 4, 5, 6, 7, 8, 9, 10, 11, 12 . . . are consecutive whole numbers.

Write down

a six consecutive **even** numbers, starting with 2.

b five consecutive **odd** numbers, starting with 1.

c four consecutive **square** numbers, starting with 1.

2 Keep the digits 1, 2, 3, 4, 5, 6, 7, 8, 9 in order and insert + and/or − signs to make a total of 100.
One way is:

$12-3-4+5-6+7+89=100$

3 Write down any 4 consecutive numbers, for example: 2, 3, 4, 5.

Multiply the two middle numbers together.
Multiply the two outside numbers together.
Repeat with different sets of 4 consecutive numbers.
What do you notice about your answers in each case?

4

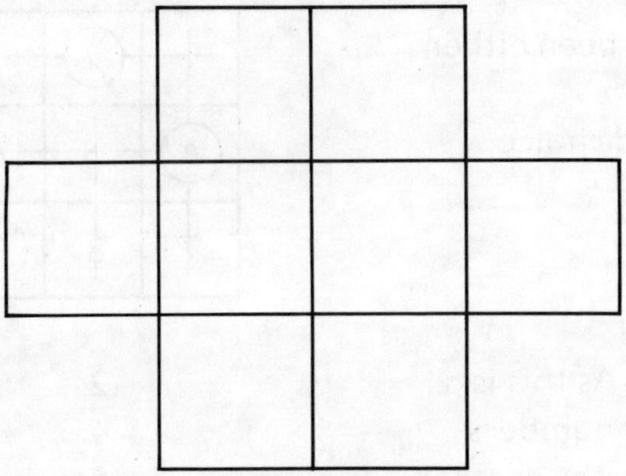

Copy the diagram and in each square place one of the numbers 1 to 8.
No two **consecutive** numbers are to be placed next to each other — vertically, horizontally or diagonally.

5 **a** Find 3 consecutive numbers which add up to 24.

b Find 3 consecutive **even** numbers which add up to 24.

c Find 3 consecutive **odd** numbers which add up to 21.

d Make up some more questions like these.

Square grids 1

The numbers 1 to 9 have been placed in the 3 × 3 square grid, starting at the top left-hand corner and going across the rows in order.

1	2	3
4	5	6
7	8	9

Select any number, put a ring round it and cross out the other numbers in the same row and column.
In this example, 2 has been chosen.

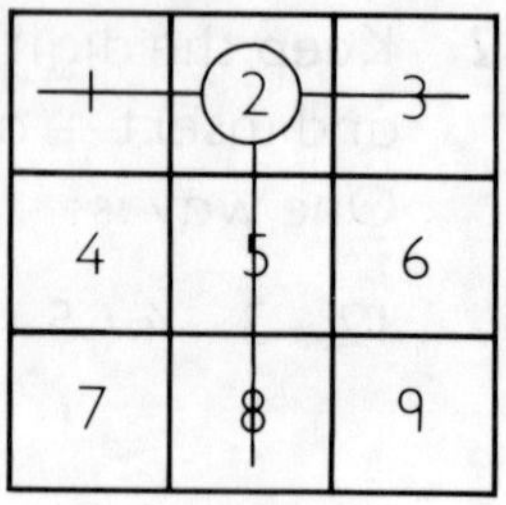

Now choose another number which has not been crossed out, put a ring round it and cross out the other numbers in the same row and column.
In the example, 4 was chosen.

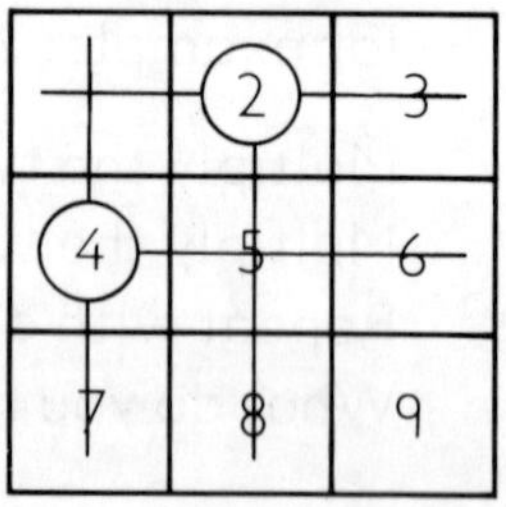

Keep doing this until all the numbers have been either ringed or crossed out.
In this example, only 9 remains as the third choice.

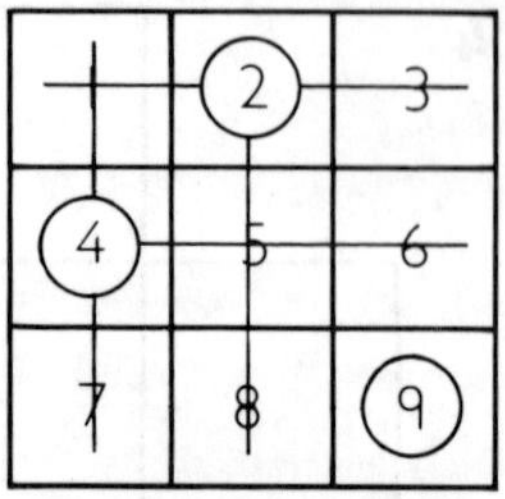

Add the numbers which have been ringed. As this is a 3 × 3 grid, divide the total by 3. Whichever numbers you choose, the final answer will always be the central number in the grid, that is 5.

$$\begin{array}{r} 2 \\ +4 \\ 9 \\ \hline 3\overline{)15} \\ 5 \end{array}$$

Try choosing other numbers in the grid to see if it always works.

Does it still work with other consecutive numbers?
For example try 6, 7, 8 ...... 14.

Square grids 2

1 Try a 5 × 5 grid with the numbers 1 to 25 written in order as before.
What is the central number this time?
What will you divide the total by this time?
Does it always work?

1	2	3	4	5
6	7	8	9	10
11	12	13	14	15
16	17	18	19	20
21	22	23	24	25

2 Try a 7 × 7 grid with the numbers 1 to 49.
What is the central number this time?
What will you divide the total by?

1	2	3	4	5	6	7
8	9	10	11	12	13	14
15	16	17	18	19	20	21
22	23	24	25	26	27	28
29	30	31	32	33	34	35
36	37	38	39	40	41	42
43	44	45	46	47	48	49

3 If the grid has an **even** number of squares along its sides, there will not be a central square.

Use the same steps as before on the numbers 1 to 16 in a 4 × 4 grid.

Remember this time the total will be divided by 4.

What is the final answer this time?
Can you explain it?

1	2	3	4
5	6	7	8
9	10	11	12
13	14	15	16

4 Try 6 × 6, 8 × 8 and 10 × 10 grids.

Anagrams and 'Odd man out'

1 The words in capital letters form an anagram of a single mathematical word. The other words give a clue.
For example: 'LARGE TIN with three sides' would be TRIANGLE.

a NAIL A DOG across the corners.

b NOT QUITE a fair share.

c DETER MICE with this length.

d ARK GO SLIM despite the weight, but . . .

e GRACE'S MOTH is lighter.

f RADAR ALL QUIET on all four sides.

g MINCE STREET is not very long.

h REST MY CLAIM on both sides of the line.

i RIPPLE AND CURE the upright.

j SO LESS ICE on equal legs.

k QUIET NAVEL is the same as silent tummy.

l I CAN LIMIT PLUTO to his table.

m ALL ARE QUIET for balanced sides.

n GET LANCER to frame a picture.

Make up some more mathematical anagrams for yourself.

2 Which do you think is the 'odd man out' in each of the following?
Write down your reason in each case.

pear, banana, poodle, peach

2, 6, 42, 49

32, 16, 48, 7

Choose another 'odd man out' for each set and give your reasons.

Place value I

1 Jeremy and Ruth were each given a number of coloured pencils for their birthday. In this diagram, each has laid out the same number of pencils, either loose or in boxes. Jeremy has three full boxes and Ruth has two full boxes. Each full box contains the same number of pencils. How many pencils are there in a box?

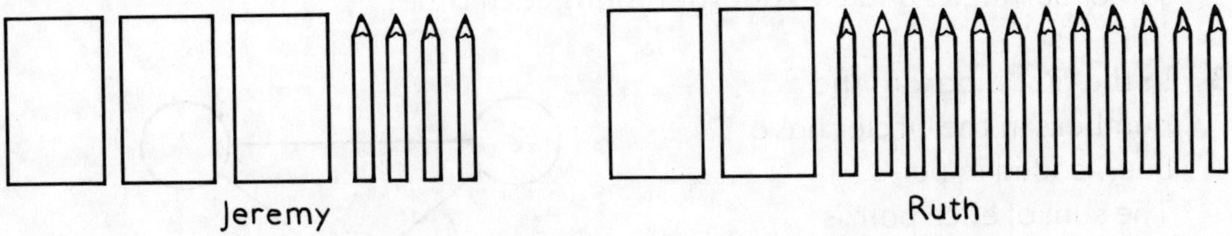

Make up a similar problem.

2 John is using lolly sticks to make shapes.

When he makes triangles he uses all the sticks.
When he makes squares he has 2 over.
When he makes pentagons he has 3 over.
How many sticks does he have?
Is there more than one answer?

3 David has more than 10 but fewer than 30 sweets.
When he counted them in fours, he had two left over.
When he counted them in fives, he had one left over.
How many sweets did he have?

4 Anne has fewer than 40 sweets.
When she counted them in sixes, she had three left over.
When she counted them in sevens, she had four left over.
How many sweets did she have?

Numbers 3

1 Take the numbers 1 to 10. Divide them into five pairs so that one pair adds up to 6, one pair adds up to 7, one pair to 9, one pair to 16, and one pair to 17.

2 The number 46 can be made using the digits 1, 2, 3 and 4 and two addition signs since $3+42+1=46$. How many other numbers can you make using the same four digits and two addition signs each time?

3 In the first diagram the numbers in the circles have been added in pairs. The sum of each pair is written beside the line joining them.

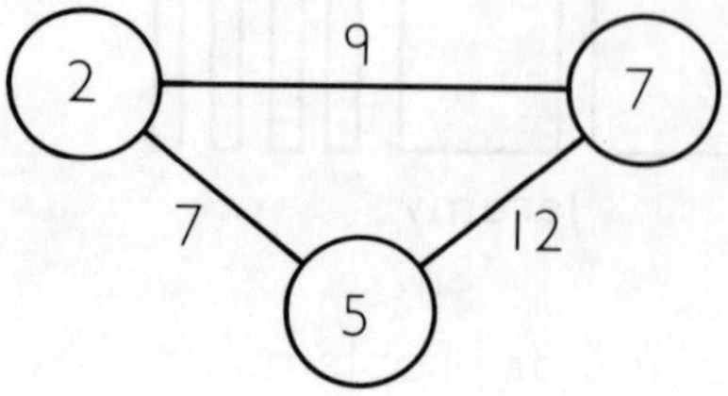

On these diagrams only the sum of each pair of numbers is shown. Find the numbers missing from the circles.

a

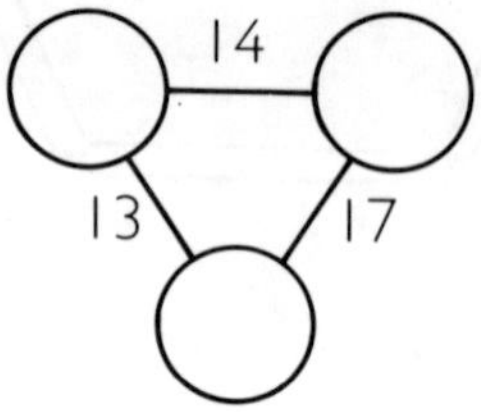

b

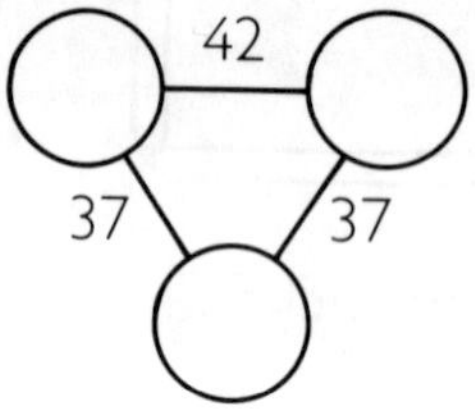

c

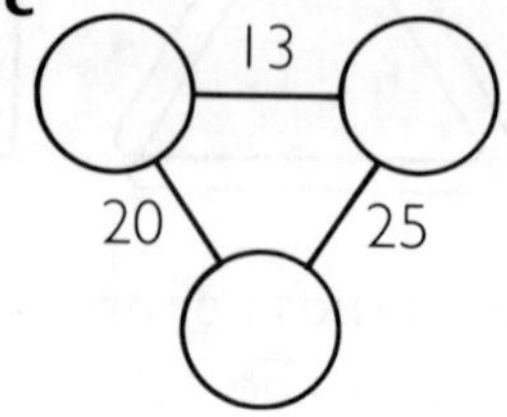

d

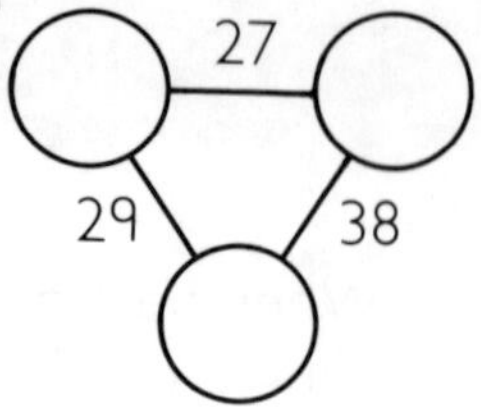

4 Add vertically to find answers **a**, **b**, **c** and **d**.
Add these answers to give the grand total, **g**.
Add horizontally to find answers **e** and **f**.
Check that **e**+**f**=**g**.

13	8	11	7	**e**
14	17	12	16	**f**
a	**b**	**c**	**d**	**g**

Now draw another grid the same shape as the first. Use the same grand total, **g**, as before but work out *different* numbers to go in the other boxes.

Shapes 2

1 Complete the alphabet putting the letters in the correct row:

A				E	F		H	I		K
	B		D			G			J	
		C								

2 How many triangles in the pentagon?

Can you invent a way to help you count them?

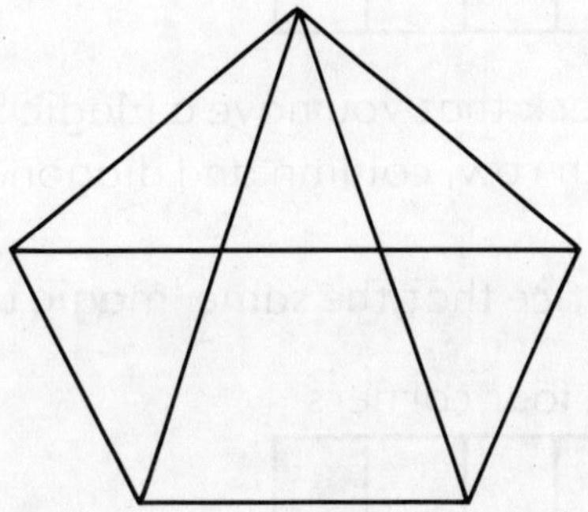

3 Pennies on the square

Draw a 4 by 4 square grid like this, but larger.

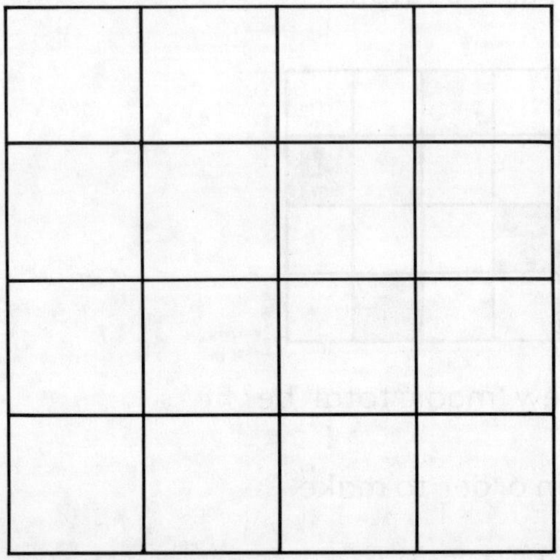

Place four pennies in the squares of the grid so that no penny is in line with another penny horizontally, vertically or diagonally.

No square may have more than one penny in it.

Now try to place five pennies on a 5 by 5 square grid . . . and six pennies on a 6 by 6 square grid, in the same way.

The 4 × 4 Magic Square

1 Write the numbers 1 to 16 in consecutive order across the rows in a 4 × 4 grid.

1	2	3	4
5	6	7	8
9	10	11	12
13	14	15	16

→

Interchange diagonally the corner cells of the outside square and the corner cells of the inside square.

16	2	3	13
5	11	10	8
9	7	6	12
4	14	15	1

Check that you have a Magic Square by adding each row, column and diagonal.

2 Notice that the same 'magic total' of 34 is given by:

the four corners

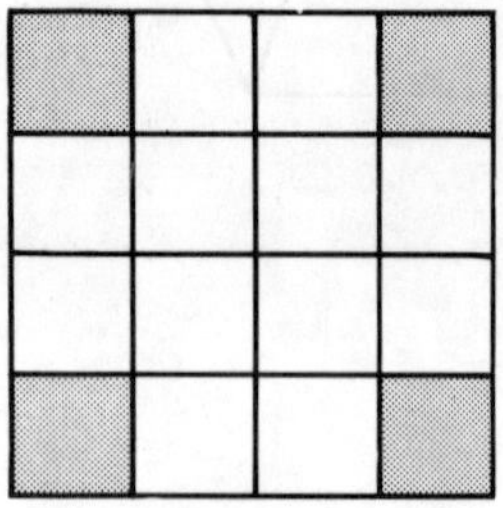

and the 'inner square'

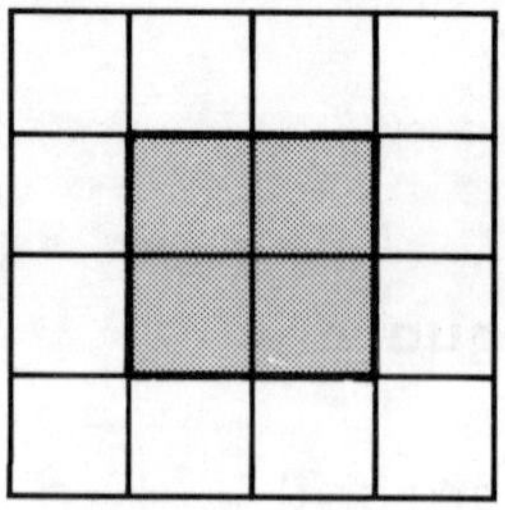

Investigate other patterns which give 34 as the total.
For example:

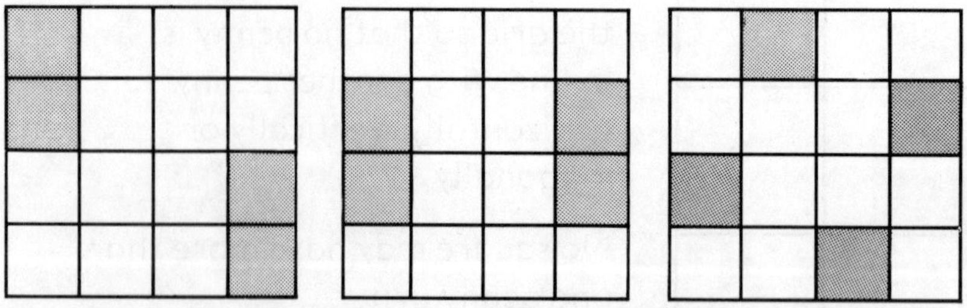

3 If 1 is added to each cell, what will the new 'magic total' be?

4 How can the Magic Square be changed in order to make the 'magic total' 50?

The 5 × 5 Magic Square and the Mathemagic Square

1 Copy and complete this 5 × 5 Magic Square.

17	24	1		15
	5	7	14	16
4	6		20	22
10		19	21	3
11	18	25		9

What is the 'magic total'?

2 Investigate other patterns which give the same total.
For example:

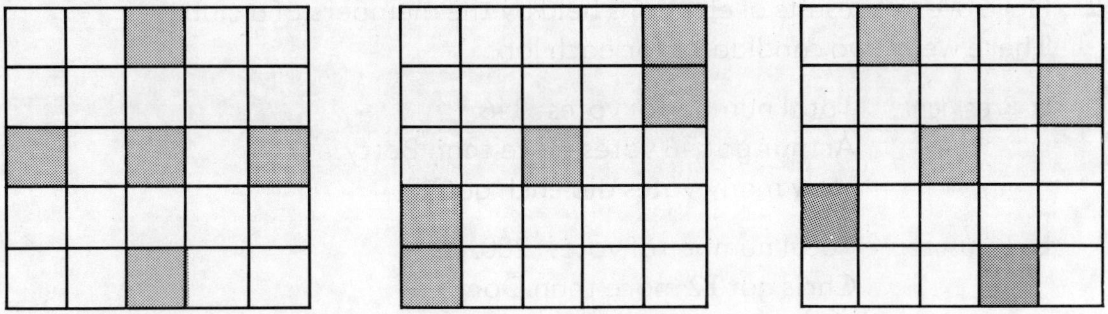

3 Copy and complete the Mathemagic Square.
Now turn it upside down and see what happens!

96		89	68
	69	91	
61		18	99
19	98	66	

Numbers 4—differences

1 Draw a small square (the inside one) and put a number at each corner. (For example: 4, 10, 7, 8).

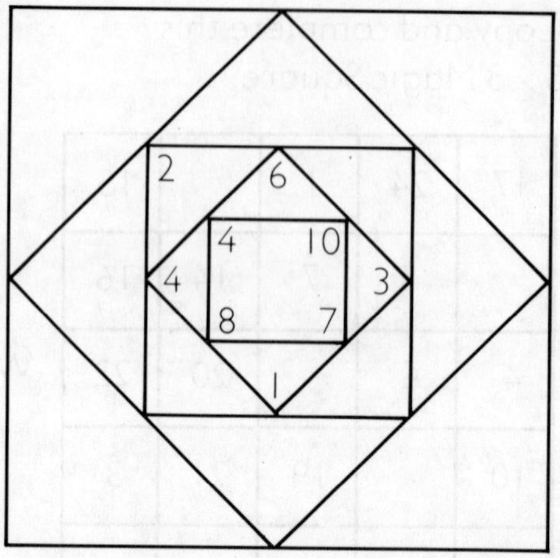

Find the difference between numbers at adjacent corners.

Each difference forms the corner of a new square, outside the first.

Keep doing this until . . . what happens?

Start again with different numbers in the corners.

2 Here are the results of elections held by the members of a club. There were two candidates for each job.

a *President:* Total number of votes: 346.
Arthur got 46 votes more than Betty.
How many votes did each get?

b *Treasurer:* Total number of votes: 280.
Chris got 72 more than Don.
How many votes did each get?

c *Secretary:* Total number of votes: 271.
Edna got 23 more than Fay.
How many votes did each get?

d Who received the most votes and who got the greatest majority? Explain these two answers.

3 In order to make a number up to 500, I need 5 more than the difference between 178 and 424.

What is the number?

Shapes 3 — cross puzzles

1 You will need to cut out six crosses like this one from squared paper.

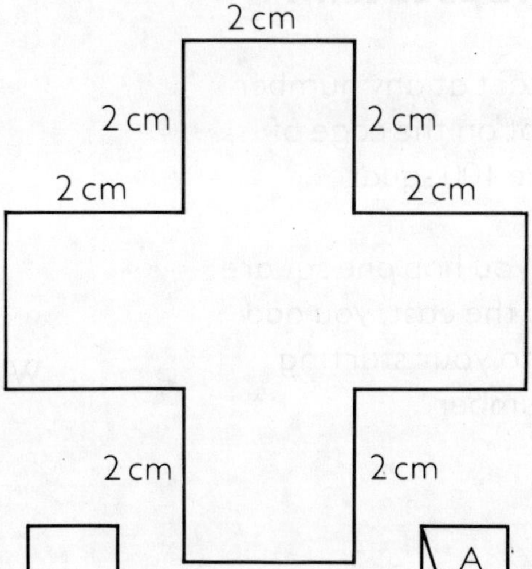

a Before you start, think about the best way to cut out the crosses so that you waste as little paper as possible.

b What is the area of one cross?

2 **a** Take two of the crosses. Cut one of them as shown in the diagram Make a square from the five pieces marked A.

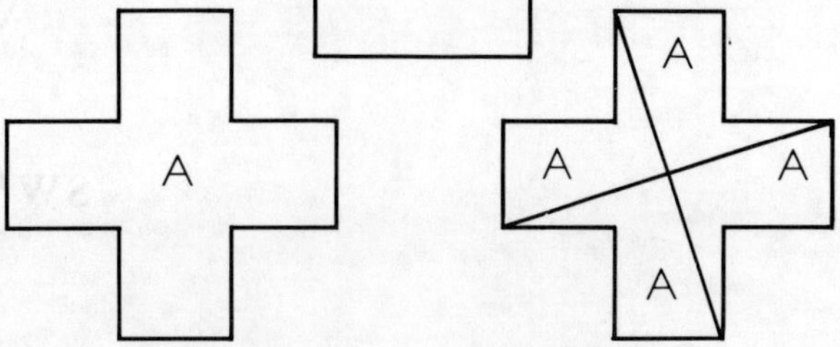

b What is the area of the square you made?

3 **a** Take another two crosses. Cut them as shown in the diagram. Make a square from the four pieces marked B.

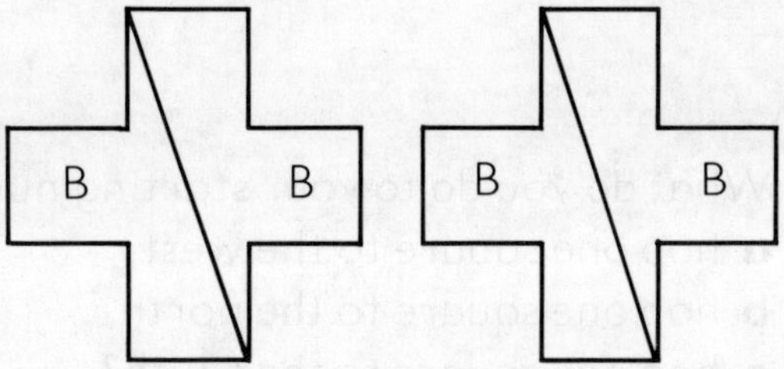

b What is the area of the square?

4 **a** Cut the fifth cross as shown in the diagram. Make a square from the four pieces marked C.

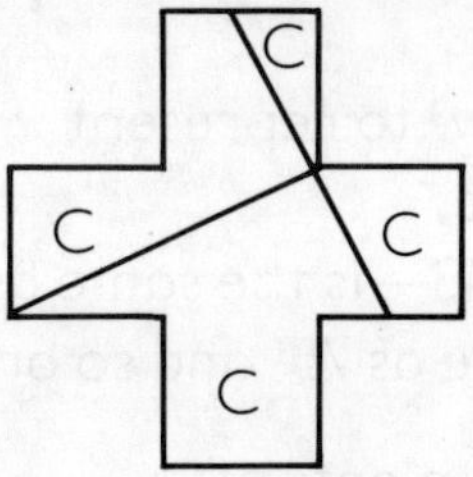

b What is the area of the square?

5 **a** Cut the sixth cross as shown in the diagram. Make a square from the four pieces marked D.

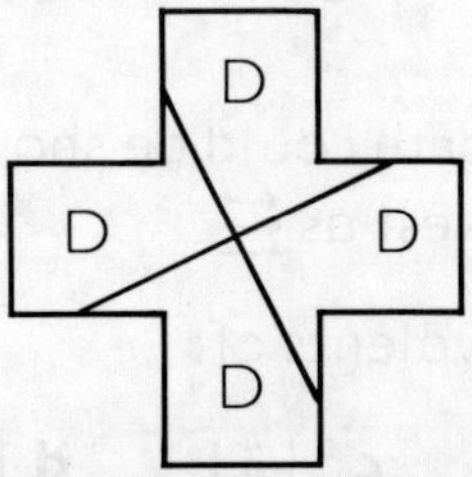

b What is the area of the square?

Hopscotch I

Start at any number not on the edge of the 100 square.

If you hop one square to the east, you add 1 to your starting number.

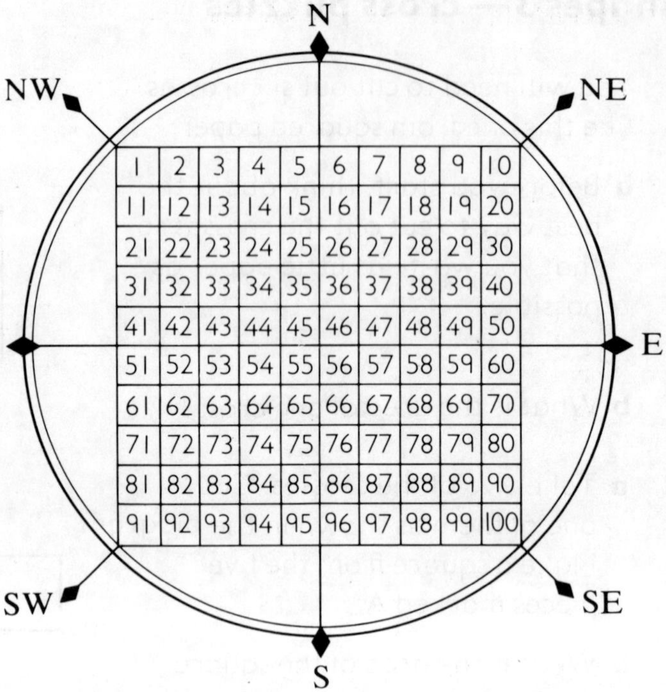

1	2	3	4	5	6	7	8	9	10
11	12	13	14	15	16	17	18	19	20
21	22	23	24	25	26	27	28	29	30
31	32	33	34	35	36	37	38	39	40
41	42	43	44	45	46	47	48	49	50
51	52	53	54	55	56	57	58	59	60
61	62	63	64	65	66	67	68	69	70
71	72	73	74	75	76	77	78	79	80
81	82	83	84	85	86	87	88	89	90
91	92	93	94	95	96	97	98	99	100

1 What do you do to your starting number if you:
a hop one square to the west,
b hop one square to the north,
c hop one square to the south?

2 Using a small arrow to represent a hop of one square, we could say that 43→is the same as 44 and 76←is the same as 75, and so on.

What are the equivalents of:

a 89→ **b** 28← **c** 54↓ **d** 74↑ **e** 19← **f** 32↑?

3 Two hops to the north could be shown as ↑↑ and 3 hops to the west as ⬱

What are the equivalents of:

a 2⇉ **b** 47⬱ **c** 51↓↓ **d** 100↑↑↑ **e** 39⬱ **f** 67↓↓↓?

Hopscotch 2

Arrows can show hops in these directions too:

north-east ↗
south-east ↘
south-west ↙
north-west ↖

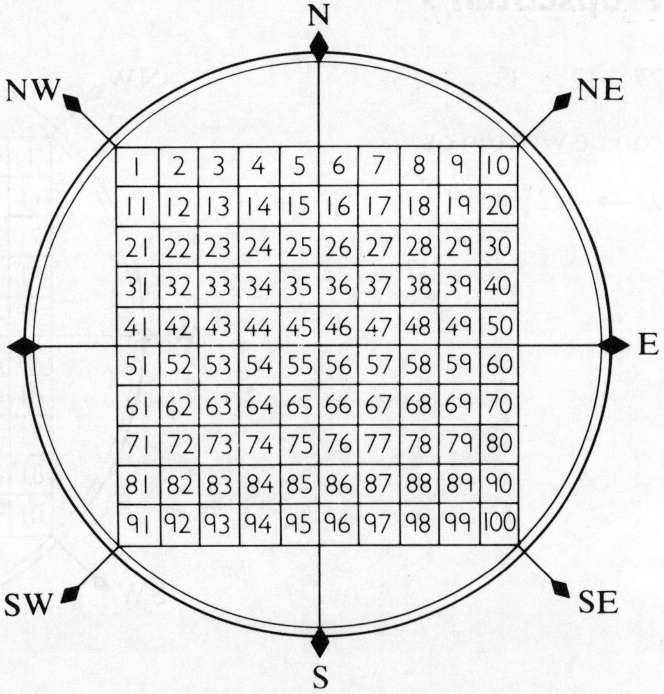

1	2	3	4	5	6	7	8	9	10
11	12	13	14	15	16	17	18	19	20
21	22	23	24	25	26	27	28	29	30
31	32	33	34	35	36	37	38	39	40
41	42	43	44	45	46	47	48	49	50
51	52	53	54	55	56	57	58	59	60
61	62	63	64	65	66	67	68	69	70
71	72	73	74	75	76	77	78	79	80
81	82	83	84	85	86	87	88	89	90
91	92	93	94	95	96	97	98	99	100

1 What are the equivalents of:

a 91 ↗ **b** 84 ↖ **c** 50 ↙↙ **d** 22 ↘↘ **e** 18 ↙↙ **f** 66 ↖↖↖ ?

2 Copy and complete:

Increasing arrows: → [+1] ↓ [ ] ↘ [ ] ↙ [ ]

Decreasing arrows: ← [ ] ↑ [−10] ↖ [ ] ↗ [ ]

3 Follow this journey: 56 ⇉ ↑ ↙↙ ↖ ⬱

Which number have you reached?
Make up your own journey and write it down.

4 What do you notice about these journeys?

a 32 → ↑ ← ↓

c 24 ↘↘ ⇇ ↗↗ ⇇

b 73 ↗↗ ↓↓ ⇇

d 67 ↘ ↑↑ ⇇ ↘

Make up some more examples like these.

Hopscotch 3

27 + 12 = 39

can be written as:

26→ + 22↑ = 39

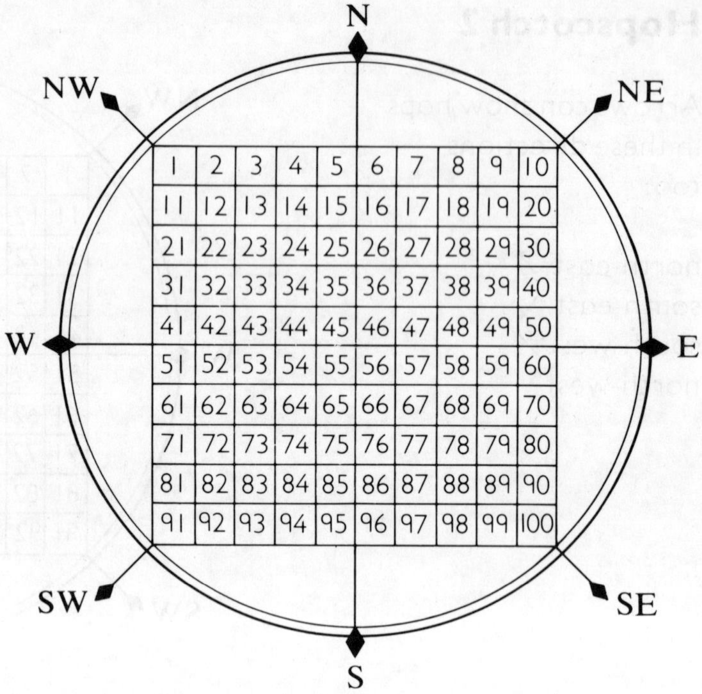

1 Work these out:

- **a** 35← + 42↑ = □
- **b** 33↘ + 44↖ = □
- **c** 82↙ + 82↑↑ = □
- **d** 98⇉ + 98↗↗ = □
- **e** the difference between 9← and 4→ is □
- **f** the difference between 19↙ and 19↖ is □
- **g** the difference between 63↓↓ and 75↑↑ is □
- **h** the difference between 100↖↖ and 1↘↘ is □

Make up some more questions like these.

2 Copy and put in the arrows:

- **a** 38← + 2□ = 49
- **b** 15□ + 19↗ = 35
- **c** 18⇇ + 33□ = 38
- **d** 5□ + 13□ = 18
- **e** 100↖ − 38□ = 41
- **f** 95□ − 28□ = 25
- **g** 16□ × 4□ = 10
- **h** 25□ ÷ 12□ = 8

Make up some more questions like these.

Money 1

1 John has one of each of these coins:

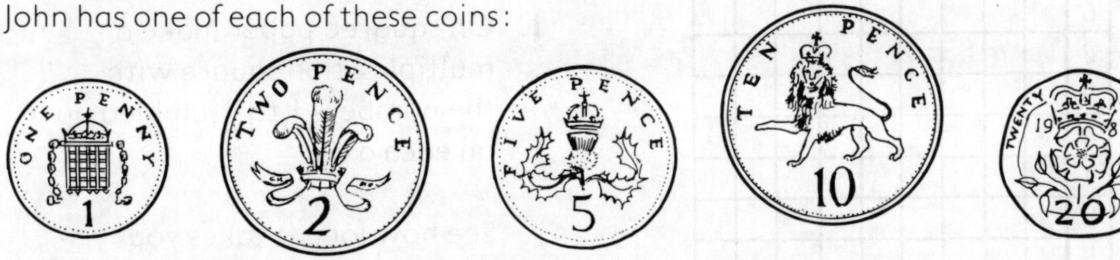

a Find the amounts less than 40p which he *cannot* make up.

b Which extra coin should I give him so that he can make up the 'missing' amounts?

c Is there another coin that would do?

2 **a** At the moment each side makes 5 pence.
Rearrange the coins so that they still form a square but the sides make 4 pence.

b Arrange three 20p coins and three 5p coins to form a triangle so that each side makes 45 pence.
Rearrange the coins to form a triangle with sides making a different total.

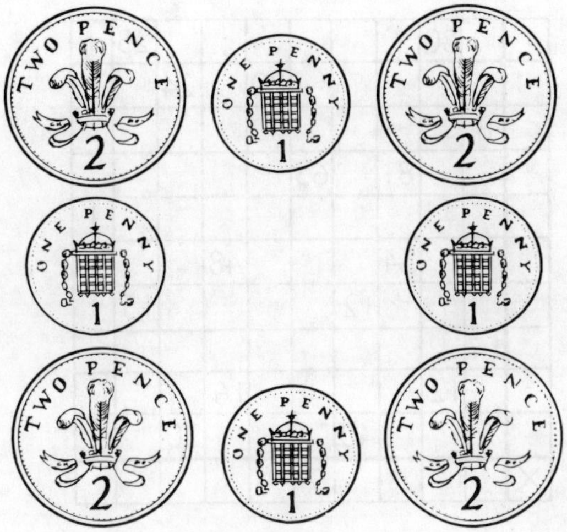

3 Here are the prices per kilogram of five different cheeses.

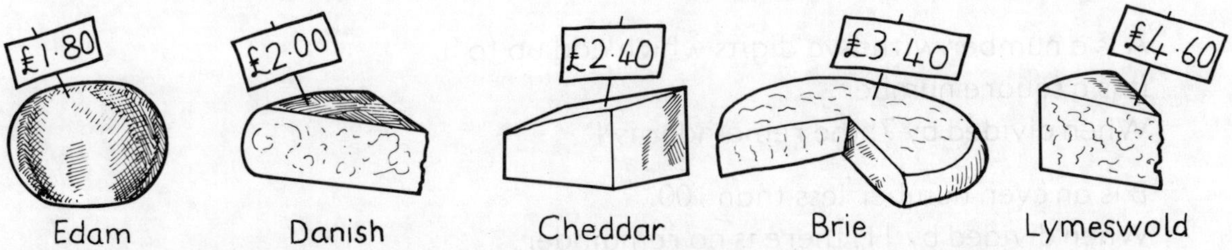

Make a ready-reckoner which will enable you to read off the cost of

1 kg 500 g 250 g 100 g 50 g

of each kind of cheese.

Use your ready-reckoner to find which costs more, 500 g of Edam or 200 g of Lymeswold.

Make up some more questions like this.

Numbers 5

6									
2									
9									
4									
1									
8									
5									
3									
7									
×	2	7	4	6	8	5	1	9	3

1 On squared paper make a multiplication square with the numbers 1 to 9 jumbled up on each axis.

See how long it takes you to fill in the square.

(Two minutes is a very good time.)

		30							25	
						80		24		
	8					40				
			81		63					
										1
			54				48			
				12					15	
	14									
		12					16			
				40				30		
×					7					

2 Here is another jumbled multiplication square.

Copy it on to squared paper.

This time use division to find all the numbers in the bottom row and the left hand column.

3 Follow the clues to find the numbers A, B and C:

A is a number with two digits which add up to 9.
It is a square number.
When divided by 7, the remainder is 1.

B is an even number less than 100.
When divided by 11, there is no remainder.
When divided by 5, the remainder is 3.

C is the smallest number which,
when divided by 4, 6 or 8,
leaves a remainder of 2.

Place value 2

1 Find the total of the numbers represented by these expressions:

five dozen
four centuries
three score and ten
two gross
a 'baker's dozen'

2 The example shows how 5 twos can be used to form a simple addition with a total of 46.

$$\begin{array}{r} 22 \\ +22 \\ 2 \\ \hline 46 \\ \hline \end{array}$$

a Use 7 sixes to form an addition with a total of 150.
b Use 7 eights to form an addition with a total of 200.
c Use 8 fours to form an addition with a total of 500.

Make up some more problems like these.

3 At a sheepdog trial there are a number of people and a number of dogs. If there are 20 heads and 66 legs altogether, how many people and how many dogs are there?
After some men take their dogs home, there are 15 heads and 50 legs.
How many men and dogs went home?

4 **a** In a playground 8 children are riding bicycles and 4 children are riding tricycles.
What is the total number of wheels?

b In another playground there are 9 children each with either a bicycle or a tricycle.
This time the total number of wheels is 23.
How many bicycles and how many tricycles are there?

c What is the connection between the total number of wheels and the number of tricycles?

Measures

1 Four children measured the length and width of a rectangular table-top to work out its perimeter. Here are the measurements they recorded:

	Length	**Width**
Anne used a metre rule.	$1\frac{1}{4}$ metres	$\frac{1}{2}$ metre
Bob used a decimetre rod.	12 dm	6 dm
Cath used a measuring tape.	1 m 21 cm	62 cm
Don used a dressmaker's tape.	122 cm	61 cm

a Work out the perimeter from each set of measurements.
b Why do you think they are not all the same?
c Which result do you think is closest to the actual perimeter?

2

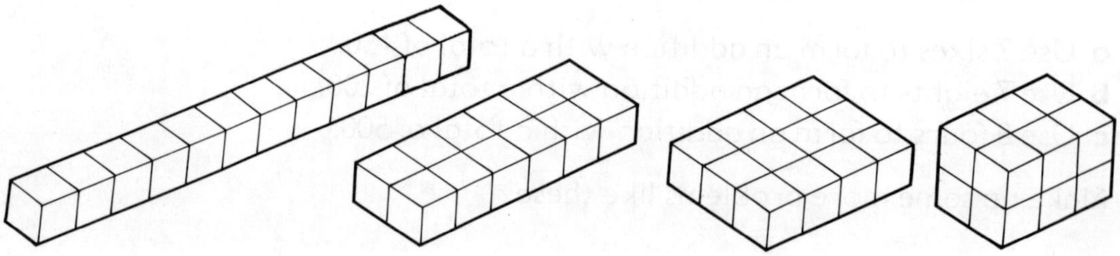

The diagrams show 4 different ways in which a cuboid can be made from 12 centimetre cubes.
These could be recorded as:

$(1 \times 1 \times 12)$ $(1 \times 2 \times 6)$ $(1 \times 3 \times 4)$ $(2 \times 2 \times 3)$

Notice that $(2 \times 3 \times 2)$ is the same as $(2 \times 2 \times 3)$ 'turned round'.

Investigate the different ways in which cuboids can be built from **a** 24 centimetre cubes and **b** 36 centimetre cubes.

3 The scales show the weight of a bottle and its contents when full of water and when half full of water.
Find the weight of the empty bottle.
What is the capacity of the bottle in millilitres?

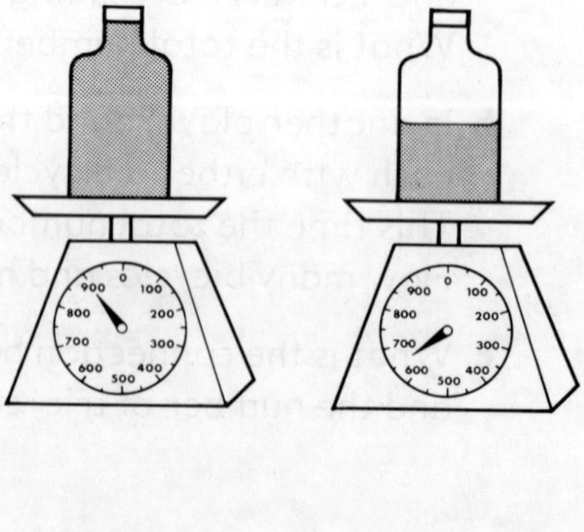

Darts I

1 To win a game of darts a total of 501 must be scored.
If Anne has scored 365, how many more must she score to win?
The scorer tells Bill, 'You need 88 to win.'
How many has Bill scored so far?
What is the difference between Anne's score and Bill's score?

2 In a game of darts each player in turn throws 3 darts. Starting at 501, the total scored by each player with 3 darts is subtracted to show what is needed to win.

Carole	David
501	501
467	436
395	397
319	306
238	241
138	156
40	42
0	

The scoreboard is shown for Carole vs. David.

a Which player won?

b How many darts did David throw in this game?

c Which player made the highest score with 3 darts?

d Find the difference between David's highest score and Carole's.

e After how many turns was David in the lead?

Darts 2

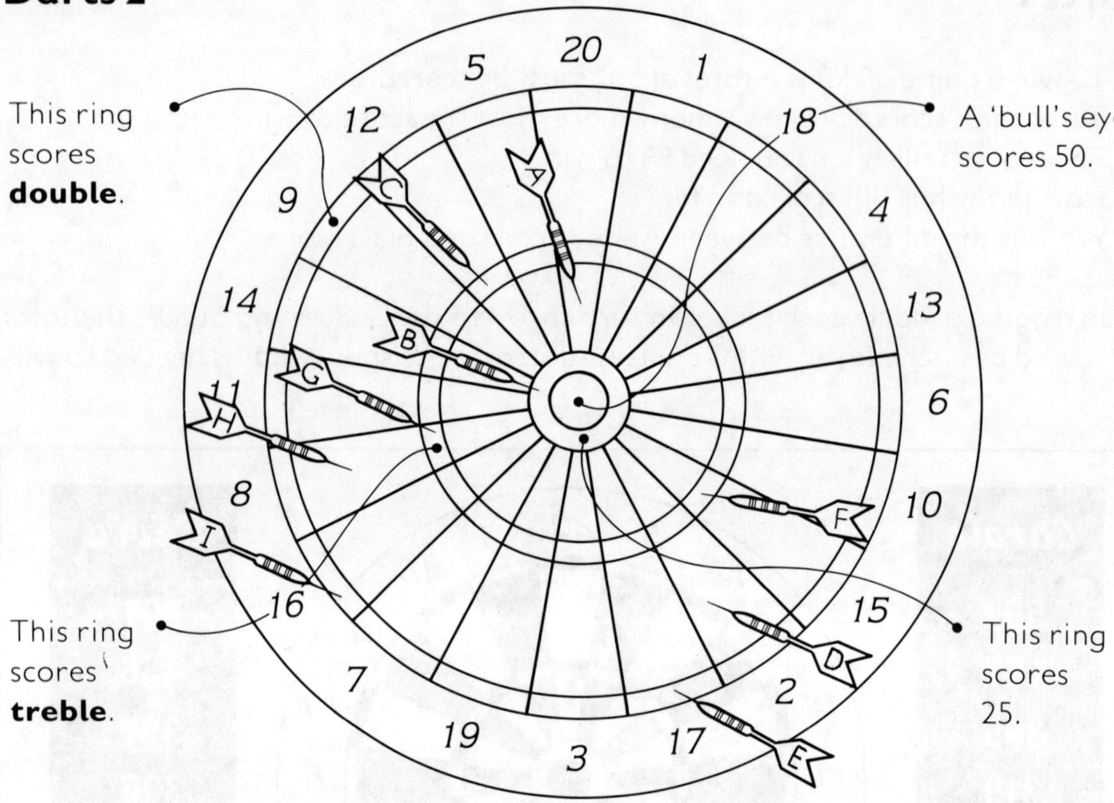

For example:

dart A	20
dart B	25
dart C (treble 12)	36
total for 3 darts	81

Find the total for each set of 3 darts:

1 D, E and F

2 G, H and I

3 'bull's eye', C and H

4 B, D and G

5 double 19, treble 3 and double 7

6 2 A's and C

Darts 3

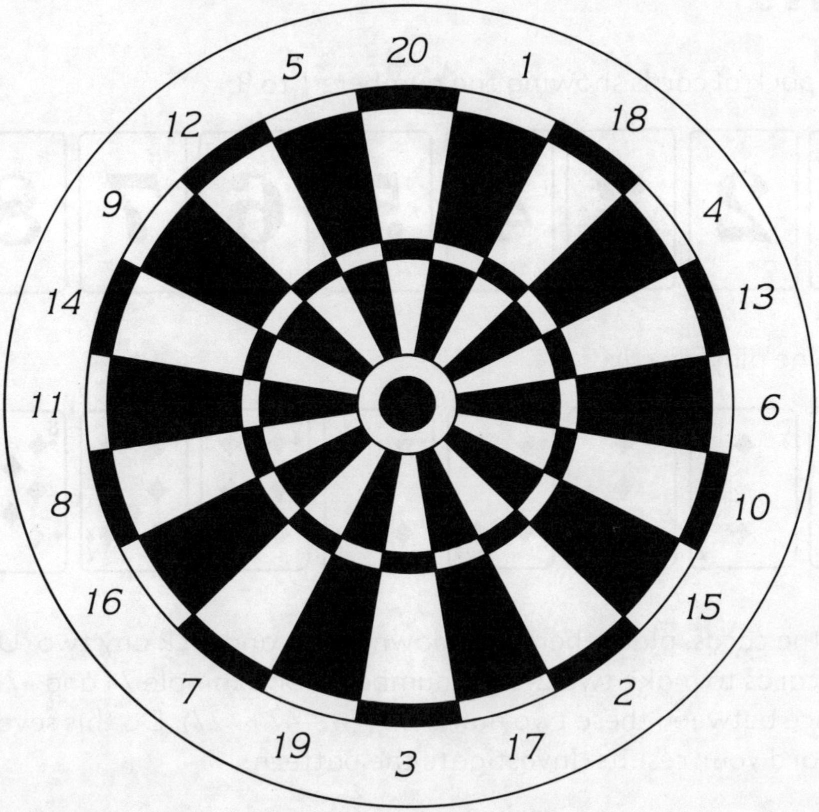

1 If 3 darts are thrown and each one scores, find:

a the highest possible score

b the lowest possible score

c 4 different ways to score 100

d how to score 159 using trebles only

e how to score 78 using doubles only

f how to score 63 with the last dart scoring a double

g how to score 148, finishing with a double

2 What is the minimum number of darts required to score 501 finishing with a double?

Numbers 6

1 Make a pack of cards showing the numbers 1 to 9:

or use nine playing cards:

Shuffle the cards, place them face downwards and pick any two. Use the chosen cards to make two 2-digit numbers, for example 74 and 47. Find the difference between these two numbers ($74 - 47 = 27$). Do this several times and record your results. Investigate the pattern.

2 A bus has 27 seats upstairs (on the top deck) and 35 inside (on the lower deck).

At the first stop 42 passengers get on the empty bus.
At the second stop 8 more passengers get on.
At the third stop 17 passengers get off and some get on.
At the fourth stop 2 passengers get off
and the conductor says, 'Only room for 6.'
How many passengers get on at the third stop?

3 Copy this table and fill in the missing numbers:

Add →

Add ↓

28	207		360
121	8	83	
201		5	316
	325		

Routes

1 The diagram represents some streets in an American city. The side of each square is 1 kilometre.

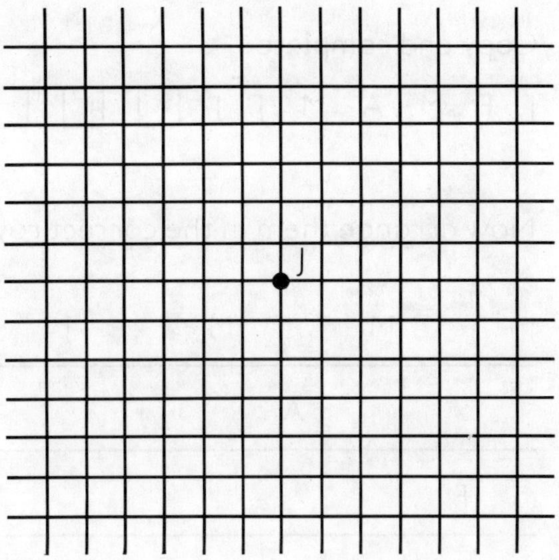

Jean lives in the corner house marked J. When she does a morning jog, she starts and ends at J without running along the same street twice.

Use squared paper to find:

a How many *different* 4 km jogs she can do.

b What shape each 4 km run traces out.

c How many *different* 6 km runs she can do and the shapes they trace out.

d Jean increases her jogs to 8 km. Investigate her routes and their 'shapes'.

2 **a** To fool robbers, a security van drives from West Devon Bank to Bloggs Factory by a different route each day. The diagram shows the streets. The side of each square is 1 kilometre. To save petrol, he must travel only 4 km on each journey. How many different routes can he take?

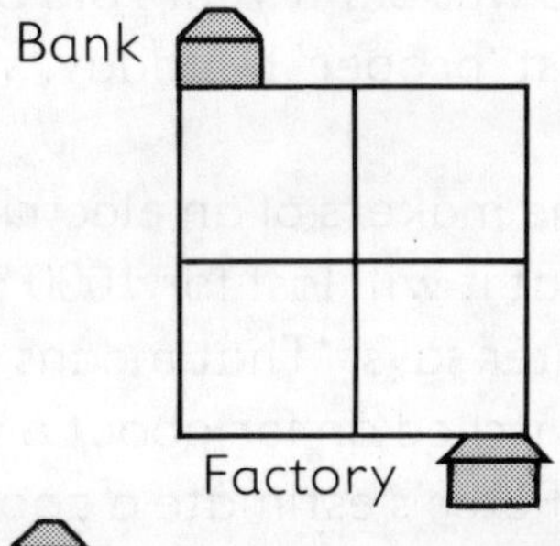

b After leaving Bloggs Factory he also has to visit the Burp Lemonade Factory. How many 6 km routes are there this time? (Warning: there are more than 15.)

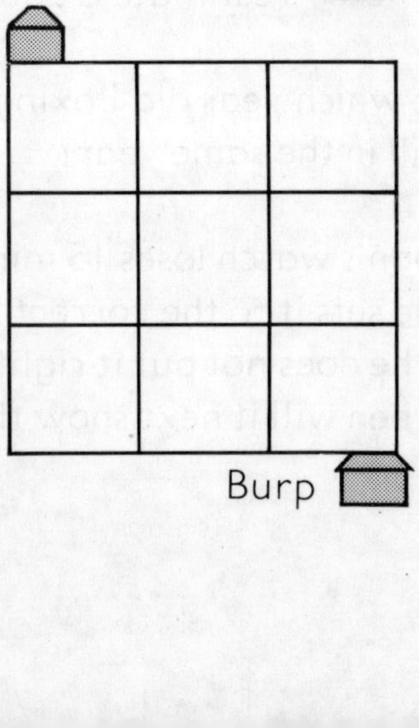

Time

1 Copy and complete:

J F M A M J J ☐ ☐ ☐ ☐ D

Now arrange them in the correct rows:

J		M		M		J
			A		J	
	F					

2 During March 1984, Anne said,
'I'm eight years old but I've only ever had two "proper" birthdays!'
On what date was Anne born?

Anne was luckier than her great-grandfather. He was eight years old before he had his first 'proper' birthday. When was he born?

3 The makers of an electric light bulb boast that it will last for 1000 hours.
Peter says, 'That means we could leave it switched on for about 6 weeks.'
Is Peter's estimate a good one?

4 In which year did Boxing Day and New Year's Day fall in the same year?

5 Don's watch loses 15 minutes every day.
He sets it to the correct time at mid-day on 1st January 1983.
If he does not put it right,
when will it next show the correct time?

Numbers 7 — letter codes

1 A, B and C are consecutive digits. Find A, B, C, and D.

Is there more than one possible solution to this problem?

$$\begin{array}{r} \text{A B C} \\ +\,\text{C B A} \\ \hline \text{D D D} \\ \hline \end{array}$$

2 Find the numbers represented by the letters in these:

$$\begin{array}{r} \text{Z} \\ +\,\text{Z} \\ \text{Z} \\ \hline \text{F Z} \\ \hline \end{array} \qquad \begin{array}{r} \text{X} \\ +\quad \text{Y} \\ \text{X Y} \\ \hline \text{Y X} \\ \hline \end{array} \qquad \begin{array}{r} \text{B A} \\ \text{B A} \\ +\,\text{B A} \\ \text{B A} \\ \hline \text{C B} \\ \hline \end{array}$$

3 Each letter represents a different number.
O represents 2 and
S represents 3.
Find the numbers the other letters represent.

$$\begin{array}{r} \text{C R O S S} \\ +\,\text{R O A D S} \\ \hline \text{D A N G E R} \\ \hline \end{array}$$

4 Each letter represents a different number.
O represents 7 and
S represents 3.
Find the numbers the other letters represent.

$$\begin{array}{r} \text{J A M E S} \\ -\quad \text{B O N D} \\ \hline \text{O O 7} \\ \hline \end{array}$$

5 If LM multiplied by LM is KLM, what numbers do K, L and M represent?

6 Each letter represents a different number
E represents 1, H represents 4 and
U represents 9.
Find the numbers the other letters represent.

$$\begin{array}{r} \text{T H R E E} \\ +\,\text{T H R E E} \\ \text{F O U R} \\ \hline \text{E L E V E N} \\ \hline \end{array}$$

Money 2

1

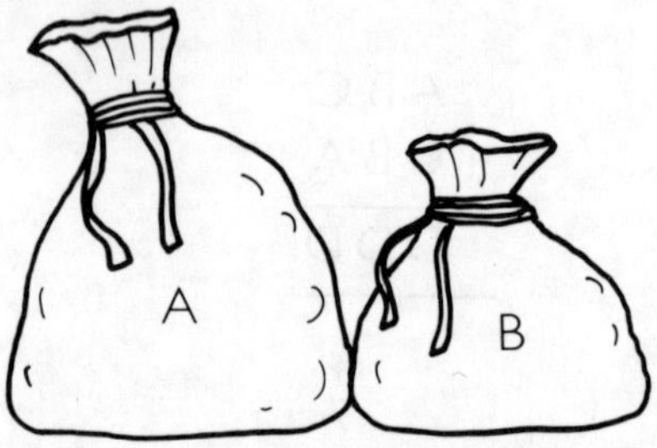

There is twice as much money in bag A as there is in bag B.

Suppose there is 20p in bag A,
then there is 10p in bag B.
The total in both bags is 30p

a If the total for both bags is 36p, how much is in each bag?
b How much is in each bag if the total is 93p?
c The total is £3.48; now how much is in each bag?
d Explain how you did questions **a**, **b** and **c**.
This diagram might help.

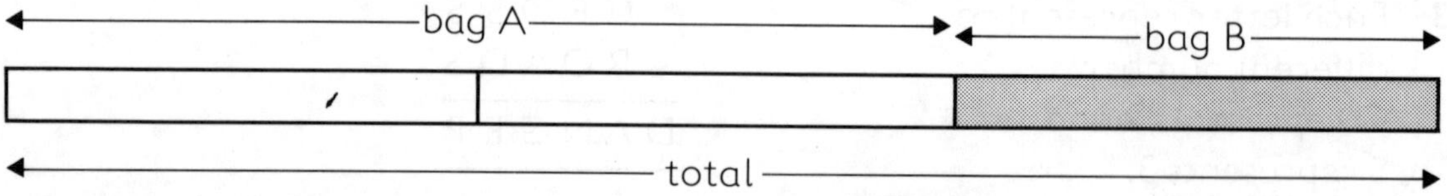

2 There is four times as much money in bag C as in bag D.

Use a diagram similar to the one in question **1** to help you find how much is in each bag if:

a the total is 50p **b** the total is 85p **c** the total is £3.20.

3 Many prices in shops end in 99p.
For example: £1.99, £3.99, £6.99, £12.99.

Why do you think shopkeepers do this?
Use a quick way to find:

a the total of the examples
b the cost of 4 at £1.99 each
c the cost of 5 at £3.99 each
d the cost of 3 at £6.99 each

Numbers 8

1 Here are some words from 'number stories' which suggest addition:
total, sum, together . . .
Find some more words to put on the list.

2 Here are some words from 'number stories' which suggest subtraction:
take away, difference, change, lost . . .
Find some more words to put on the list.

3 In the square the digits 1 to 9 are arranged so that the number in the middle row is twice the number in the top row and the number in the bottom row is three times the number in the top row.

1	9	2
3	8	4
5	7	6

Find the three other ways of arranging the digits to give the same result.

4 Here are three problems about people's ages. The first one is fairly easy.

a Ann is 5 years older than Bill. If the sum of their ages is 25, how old are they?
Think about the method you used to answer **a** and use the same method for these slightly harder problems.

b Carol is 2 years older than Denis. If the sum of their ages is 52, how old are they?

c Eve is 7 years older than Frank. If the sum of their ages is 51, how old are they?

Make up some more problems like this.

5 A mother is 32 years older than her 12 year-old daughter. She says, 'When I am three times as old as you are, I'll buy you a ring.' How long does the girl have to wait?

Place value 3

Single packets of chewing gum are packed in boxes of 12 or dozens. Twelve boxes are in turn packed in a carton so that each carton holds 12 dozen or a **gross**; that is 144 packets of chewing gum.

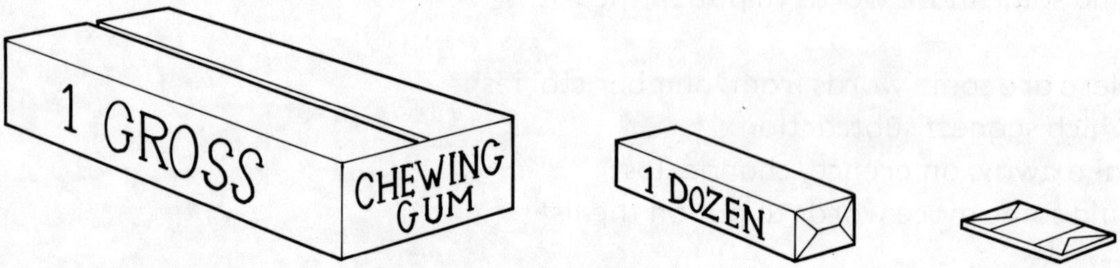

In order to record his stock of chewing gum,
Mr Munch has to use two extra digits:

X for ten and ⚹ for eleven

g	d	u	
	X	4	means ten dozen and four or 124 packets
	2	⚹	means two dozen and eleven or 35 packets
1	2	3	means one gross, two dozen and three or 171 packets

Try these problems in grosses, dozens and units (packets)

```
a    g d u        c    g d u        e    g d u
       5 3             1 6 0             2 7 8
   +   2 2         +     1 X         +     4 ⚹
       1 5               2 2               3 7
     _____             _____             _____

     _____             _____             _____

b    g d u        d    g d u        f    g d u
     1 X 9             2 4 X             5 2 4
   -   7 4         -     3 ⚹         -   X 7
     _____             _____             _____

     _____             _____             _____
```

Change all your answers to base ten numbers.

The Chinese tangram 1

Tangram puzzles were invented by the Chinese over 4000 years ago.
There are only two simple rules:
all seven pieces must be used,
the pieces must not overlap.

How to make a Chinese tangram

1 On stiff card draw a 10 cm square.
2 Draw in a diagonal.
3 Join the mid-points of two adjacent sides of the square.
(This line is parallel to the diagonal.)
4 Start to draw the other diagonal, but only as far as the line joining the mid-points.
5 Complete the small square.
6 By drawing a line parallel to the side of the big square, complete the parallelogram and the isosceles right-angled triangle.
7 Cut out all seven pieces carefully.

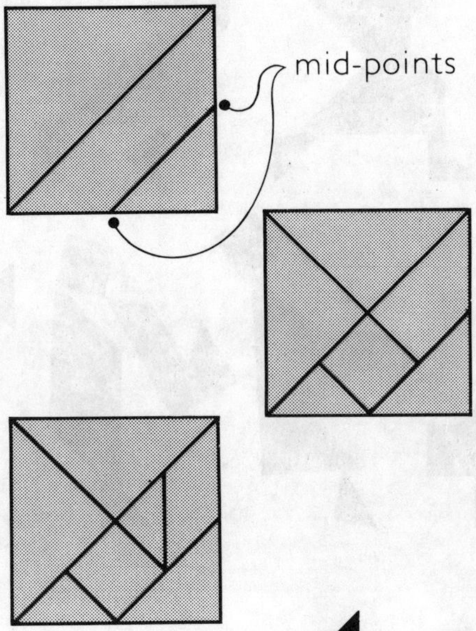

Try to make these shapes. (Remember the rules!)

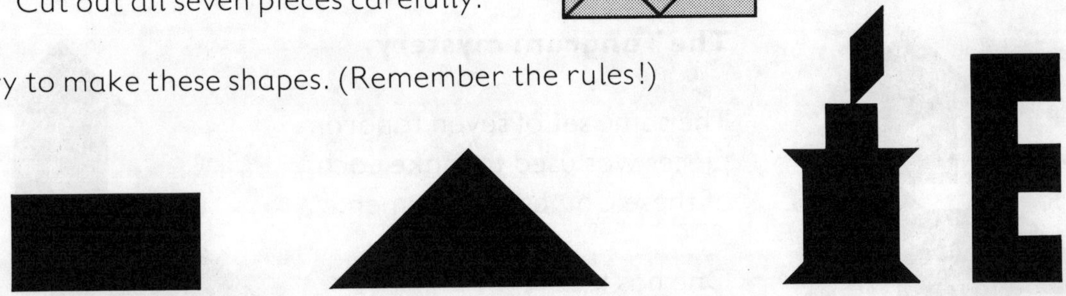

If each shape is made from a 10 cm square, what is its area?

Make some shapes of your own.

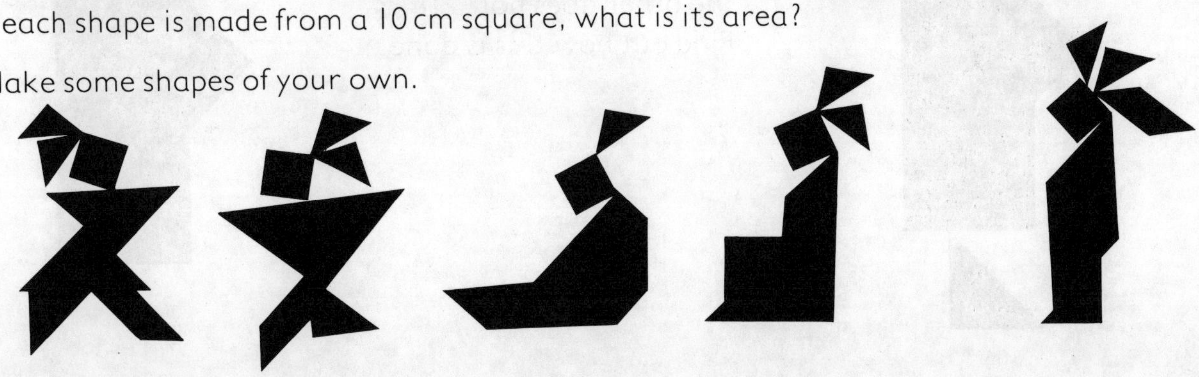

The Chinese tangram 2

Tangrams can be used
to make animals

dancers

footballers

or even
a jazzband!

The Tangram mystery

The same set of seven tangram pieces was used to make each of these Chinese gentlemen.

One has feet,
the other does not.
Find out how this is done.